Ending the COLD WAR
Between
Salesmen & Customers

By:

ANDREY SIZOV

&

JIM MATHERS

Admiral Press

ADMIRAL
PRESS

1315 Cleveland Street
Clearwater, FL 33755

Library of Congress Control # : 2015942537

ISBN : 978-1515347859

Notes from readers:

I've read the book twice. The 1st time a few days after you sent it to me and again over the weekend. I want my kids to read it since the advice is as much about life itself as it is about sales! There were quite a few chapters about goals and being honest with yourself that I've been harping on with my children since they were small – mainly due to the hard lessons their dad learned.

From a personal sales career perspective, Advice 8 - "fighting with customers," Advice 17 - about "perfect" being the enemy of "good," and Advice 14 and 39 - about speaking in the customer's language and not creating confusion, all resonated with me. Advice 40 - the 100% coefficient of efficiency will bring a smile to anyone who takes sales seriously. From an overall career perspective, I appreciated Advice 30 -Fundamentals of Success. Any reference to Mark Twain is a plus in my mind.

My biggest take away was in Advice 44 - "sales is the service provided to help the customer make the best choice" – a novel way of looking at the career.

Thank you for sending this to me.

Best of luck,

John Belgiovine,

Director of Sales,

Direct Energy

I absolutely loved this book! It has given me a whole new viewpoint on what "sales" really is! I am a single mom, I own my own business and I used to feel uncomfortable with the word "sales." I really didn't like to "sell" my customers.

The way Jim talks about the Cold War between customers and salesmen clarified for me why "sales" became a bad word. Now I know how to make "selling" an enjoyable experience for me, and my customers.

I give as much beneficial information as possible to my clients and the more I do, the more they buy from me and the happier they are.

I really feel like a champion now as I've made more sales than ever before in my life and this has resulted in more happy clients. In

just 6 months I have 10x'd my sales.
This is the best sales book I've ever read!
Thank you!!!!
Josi Valerio,
Entrepreneur

Acknowledgment

We wish to acknowledge a man whose accomplishments have withstood the test of time. He was a humanitarian, philosopher, adventurer, pragmatic scholar and supreme organizer. Hubbard® Management Technology is a gift to any business owner anywhere. For the gifts of knowledge he has given to us, we recognize L. Ron Hubbard as our best friend.

DEDICATION

This book is dedicated to Salesmen
of every sex, race, religion and political ideology
on this planet.

Salesmen
are a vital necessity
to every booming economy
on Earth.

Nearly 8 billion people have something in common:
They buy or trade some commodity -
water, food, beans, coffee, salt, computers, phones, etc.,
every single day of the year.

For ease of communication and
rapid dissemination of basic concepts,
we use the terms "he" and "salesman" in this book to refer to
any woman or man who sells any type of commodity or service.
We are less concerned with being politically correct,
and
more concerned with creating
EFFECTIVE & WEALTHY Sales Professionals!

Table of Contents

Introduction

The Cold War, a period of high tension between the two biggest Nuclear Powers on the planet, Russia and the United States, peaked in 1985. The fear of nuclear annihilation grew continuously after WWII and held the attention of every major world power. When the Berlin Wall was knocked down in 1989, marking the end of the Cold War, the whole world breathed a sigh of relief. Nuclear war, considered by experts as the *final solution*, was a war that neither side could ever really win. The one point all nations agreed upon was that all-out nuclear war would affect every other country and living thing on the planet.

The main problem of the Cold War was the constant uncertainty and distrust on both sides of the negotiating table. During the summer and fall of 1985, Russian Navy anti-submarine corvette officer, Lt. Andrey Sizov, and United States Navy submarine officer, Lt. Jim Mathers, were involved in Cold War operations in the North Atlantic Ocean that involved searching for and potentially being ordered to destroy each other.

Today, these two former Cold War enemies have joined together in peace and understanding to solve a different kind of Cold War. A Cold War that has been going on for centuries: ***the Cold War between Customers and Salesmen.***

It happens every day in every market place in the world. Customers have been pitched, run over, worn down, "sold," harassed, lied to, sucked up to, taken "care" of, or bribed for centuries. Likewise, Salesmen have been lied to, "sold," harassed, bribed, knocked down, put down, abandoned, demoralized and left in the dust. Talk to the average salesman and they will tell you: "It's a war out there." Ask the average customer and they will say: "you just can't trust a salesman."

It's an accepted rule that 20% of the salesmen make 80% of the sales. What are those successful salesmen doing right? Why are most salesmen fighting all day every day just to make a living? Why is the sales process a fight in the first place for most sales people? Why do customers feel like they need a defense? Why is it a battle? Who is winning? Are we doomed to a never ending Cold War?

Observations of two lifetimes are gathered in this book – regarding the winning attitudes of champion sales professionals and handling customers correctly with the goal of *ending* the Cold War between customers and sales professionals.

Russian business-coach and author, Andrey Sizov, and American business owner and sales trainer, Jim Mathers, disclose the principles they have proven to be the foundation of champion sales professionals. Andrey and Jim share the same basic philosophy regarding the successful actions of sales champions. They were former enemies, worlds apart, speaking different languages, but both had the exact same concept of how to train the very best salesmen. They have been teaching salesmen how to be professionals and gain the wealth they deserved by being the best in their profession for over 20 years on two different continents.

Outlined here are 55 simple and easy to understand lessons, useful for any sales professional, sales manager or sales executive, no matter how much experience they have in the field of professional sales.

Whether you are doing phone sales, door-to-door sales, retail store sales, or large commercial enterprise sales, the basic fundamentals that lead to increasing wealth and success are the same, no matter what language you speak or what country you live in.

These lessons are also extremely useful for entrepreneurs, small business owners and managers, multi-level marketers, artists and anyone who has a product or service they would like to get other people to buy.

There *is* a correct way to sell to people that leads to high customer satisfaction, high commissions and high repeat and referral sales.

Study these fundamental rules and laws, practice them every day, and if you master these, you will become a true Sales Champion and earn the wealth you deserve.

Let's make a deal:

We'll tell you what we've learned over the past 25 years.
Then you observe what is useful and interesting for you.
And you decide what lessons you will use or not.

Agreed?

Good! Let's get started!

Advice № 1
Believe... And You Will See

Let's get right to the core of the matter.

Love, Duty, Honor, Beauty, Harmony – these qualities *do* exist in life.

If it were not true, life would be a sad and dreary prospect. These ideals and their manifestations do exist in life. And those who want to see them, do, whenever and wherever they look. These qualities exist, whether you believe in them or not.

The following principle works here:

"Believe, and you will see."

If you believe these good qualities of life do exist, you will see evidence of them around you and you will use them to provide benefits to others as well as yourself. If you don't believe in them – then you won't see them and these qualities won't exist in your life. If you believe that people are only out for themselves, and it's a "dog eat dog" world, then you won't see these ideals, and as a result, you won't attract these honorable qualities for the benefit of yourself and others.

Decide for yourself. It's your choice. You're at a train station and you can go in two different directions. Where do you want to go? Only you can decide for yourself. If you truly don't believe that Love, Honor, Duty, Faith, Beauty and Harmony exist, put this book down, because this book is based on that foundation. We will tell you about the train that drives toward success and true wealth, which is always with you; you shouldn't have to chase after money as the only goal and stress yourself out every day. Choose wisely.

The stars shine only for those who look up at the night sky.

Advice № 2
Be Yourself or Pretend?

You are very able and you have a huge potential of success.
You were born wealthy and successful!
This is your natural condition.

Maybe you have been taught that you are not wealthy or successful and you have to "pretend" to be something you're not in order to be successful and rich. This pretense causes stress and tension.

Be who you actually are!

If you don't have everything working perfectly yet, just admit to yourself: "It's not perfect yet." As long as you continue to practice and learn to be a true professional, you will start to be perfect more often. "Be yourself" wholeheartedly without trying to be more or less than you are. Don't pretend to be something you are not.

Some people, misunderstanding this law, try to create a false picture of success. This causes a lot of stress. They may "seem" happy and wealthy and even try hard to "believe" it. They try to convince others, and spend a lot of their attention and time in this effort. They act nice and kind to a customer only because they want the money, not because they want to help the customer.

This false pretense really becomes obvious when the customer suddenly decides that he is not going to buy. The salesman sees the sale is lost and thinks, "That's it, there's no more reason to pretend to be a polite person; now I can be myself." At that moment, the customer will notice a change in his attitude and will hear less flattering remarks from the salesman who is no longer "pretending" to be polite.

Stress and tension occur because of the desire to show others an attitude that actually doesn't exist inside. This causes strong turmoil and discomfort inside the salesman. Over time he will stop selling as much as he was before or just quit that job. And, he will find and give different reasons to "explain" why he quit selling; the company is bad, the sales manager is bad, the commission plan is unfair, etc.

The idea is simple:
To have more success and money in sales,
BE who you really are,
and stop working under so much stress and strain.

This works in any area of life, not just sales.

We will show you precisely how this occurs and what you can do to avoid this stress and strain easily and effectively.

Advice № 3
What You Should Do If You Want More

Realize that if you want to have more (sales, money, time, etc.) than you have now,
you should do something *different* from what you are currently doing.

Your daily actions need to change.

And you need to consistently do these new actions, if you want more success.

And this, as a rule, is something unusual and is connected with breaking out of your current "comfort zone." And it will take some effort and practice to break out!

Any new and better goal is *always* located *outside* your comfort zone.

Always.

To achieve any new goal requires persistent effort (if it were easy, you would see everyone around you achieving new goals every day). So, in order to really break out of your current comfort zone, you need to be willing to work harder than everyone else in order to live a more happy and wealthy life than before. This is not as difficult as it may seem at first.

Everything new and worthwhile seems difficult until it becomes easy as you learn the secret of how to do it.

You have to ask yourself if you really want to be successful.

Do you really want to be a rich and successful sales professional?

Be honest with yourself.

Be willing to change your mind.

It is a lot more fun being able to buy your friends dinner without having to worry about paying for rent.

Advice № 4
How Champions Win

Champions win by constantly battling toward their goal, especially at the beginning stage. And they never get upset if their first attempts are unsuccessful. They achieve success because they don't quit moving toward their goal.

This is the way to **Win** in life and sales:

To win, it's more important to keep moving forward toward your goal. Don't worry about making mistakes. True success lies in the willingness to keep trying, learning from any mistakes, and moving forward no matter how small some of the steps you take may be. Keep moving forward! Don't quit! Don't fall back into the comfort zone of mediocrity.

Jim's experience:
When I founded my energy sales company in the summer of 1999, the first three clients I signed up failed to pay for my services. I was running the company at a loss for the first three months. My first son was just born, and my wife was worried, but very encouraging. I kept telling her everything would be okay.

I didn't take my eye off my goal, and I worked harder to find the right client.

I did find an amazing client.

And I made my first million dollars as a result of not giving up on my goal.

Advice № 5
Champions Definition of "Sales"

Here is the definition of "Sales" that champions use:

Sales is the service of helping a customer choose the BEST product or service.

True sales success is defined as helping so many people make the best choice that the number of customers who buy is more than anyone else expects to be humanly possible.

Advice № 6
The Target of the Champion

The target of the wealthy and successful sales-champion is NOT trying to high pressure close every single potential customer, hunting them down and forcing them into a decision without their understanding and agreement.

The real target is EASY!

Just keep talking to a LOT of different people – and talking to warm prospects more frequently – keep honoring their right "to choose" and then help them to decide "to buy or not to buy," and if the decision is "to buy," then help them decide "what exactly" to buy. If the customer decides not to buy, respect that decision, don't assume the door is closed forever, and keep finding ways to help them understand what they really need and show them how to get it.

A sales rep that clings desperately to each and every potential customer (trying to be "liked" by them) will accumulate a lot of internal negativity and will eventually stop trying completely.

Real success means continuous pleasure with your work and the willingness to talk to more and more people.

Andrey's Coat Collar:

In 1988 I was going through ship commander training and I needed to get a rare lambskin collar for my overcoat. Real Russian Navy officers were incredibly competent and willing to do any job in any climate, with complete disregard for any barriers or regulations. And Real Russian Navy officers were also the most classy and stylish rogues imaginable. In short, Real Russian Navy officers wore rare lambskin collars, banned by regulations, which meant I really had to have one.

I went to every tailor in St Petersburg. Not one offered that collar. This was a big problem for a young man looking to fit the role of a Real Russian Navy officer.

Luckily, I mentioned my problem to a real estate agent, who taught me the first target of a sales champion – EVERYBODY MUST KNOW THAT YOU ARE SELLING (or buying) SOMETHING! Everybody must know that you have something valuable to offer. I thought it would be weird and uncomfortable to tell everybody I met that I needed a rare collar for my naval overcoat. As if he read my mind, he said: "Yes, this is the biggest problem for salesmen - considering the action of talking to very many people uncomfortable and embarrassing."

"It simply means that everybody must know what you do. YOU CONTINUE TALKING TO MANY MANY PEOPLE AND KEEP LOOKING FOR THE BEST WAYS TO INTRODUCE WHAT YOU DO. You will get better and better at it. Just remember the trick is to get people curious about what you are doing."

I applied this principle to my problem. I told all my friends and acquaintances what I was looking for; some thought I was crazy and laughed at me and others had no idea how to help me. Finally, I told my Mom and her friends. She looked at me and asked if I was aware that she was a chief economist at a respectable company and neither she nor her respectable friends had any interest at all in collars and navy coats. So, I told those "respectable" ladies a story. I explained the difference between staff navy officers (those who never had to go to sea) and Real Russian Navy officers who actually went to sea and chased American submarines around the North Atlantic, and why it was a matter of honor to wear this special collar. They became curious and started asking questions.

IF YOUR STORY IS INTERESTING, PEOPLE WILL LISTEN TO YOU. PEOPLE LOVE INTERESTING STORIES AND TELLING STORIES ALLOWS YOU TO ATTRACT MORE ATTENTION TO YOUR PROJECT.

After 2 days of telling everyone I ran into about the special collar I was looking for, I started to receive advice from many different people, including people I had never even met.

After 2 weeks of telling my story to everyone I met, a man I met on a train the very first day I applied this lesson called and told me he found the place that sold the special collar I needed. I thanked him, bought the collar and proudly wore it to show everyone I was a "Real" Russian Navy officer.

Advice № 7
When Selling Becomes a Serious Battle

If a sales rep doesn't honor the customer's right to choose – "to buy or not to buy" – he automatically gets into a fight. What fight? A "Cold War." No punches are thrown. But, the customer is fighting for his freedom to choose and the sales rep fights against that freedom. Whether the sales rep understands it's a battle or not, he becomes tired of fighting. Why? It's not easy to fight all the time! As a result, the work becomes serious, hard and eventually unbearable.

It really is very simple:

"Please, come in and look at what we have to offer. If you see something you like, we will be very happy to help you. Don't buy anything you don't need. There's no rush, we don't want you to make the wrong choice. A wrong choice is more expensive for our company. And to help you make the best choice for you, we have professionals whose main purpose is to save you from buying things you don't need. They are happy to do their job."

The phrases vary but the main idea is always exactly the same. Anyone can be trained to do this. You just direct the attention of your managers, consultants and sales professionals to this main point of servicing the customer's needs first. It has been proven time and again, that more money, customers and pleasure come as a result in those companies where this is done correctly.

Advice № 8
Rule of Success in Sales

If you fight with the customer, <u>not</u> allowing him to "choose *not* to buy your product," you will become tired, and sooner or later you will cease to love your job.

<u>RULE:</u>
Help your customer, by giving him the correct information to make the best choice and allowing him the right to <u>not</u> buy your product, and you won't become tired, you won't strain yourself, you will enjoy working with more people, and best of all, you won't be "fighting" your customers.

By practicing this attitude and doing this consistently, you will become a Sales Champion.

Of course, nothing written here cancels the need for you to *persist* in providing enough information to make your customer interested in your product or service, as well as to create the desire to buy and then to receive the payment.

As you continue to practice, your ability to comfortably persist with every single person will grow. And the percentage of those who buy your product or service will rise higher and higher, while the effort and strain you feel will become less and less. You should always try for 100% closing rate. But there is **no** sales champion who can honestly say: "I close every single person I talk to." He doesn't worry about closing every single one. This is why the champion has the highest closing rate, the highest commission, and the biggest smile.

<u>Andrey's first experience in the United States:</u>
I visited a shoe store in Los Angeles, California, during my first trip to the United States. I wasn't going to buy anything, I just wanted to know what style of shoes people wear in America, and I wanted to see how Americans *sell*. I tried on two pairs of shoes, but they didn't fit

and asked for a third pair with a guilty look because I didn't want to waste the salesman's time. When the third pair didn't fit me, I hesitantly asked for a fourth pair and the salesman suddenly understood what was happening:

- *"Are you from Russia?"*

- *"Yes."*

- *"Then please wait a second."*

The salesman brought someone to translate for us and then he began to explain as if taking extra care of Russian customers was part of his normal routine:

- *"I want to clear something up for you, Sir, or I just won't be able to help you. You are the CLIENT here. You can touch everything and try anything on. If you are still here after closing time, we will wait for you. The main thing is, if you don't want to buy anything, that's really ok. You have the freedom to buy or not to buy. Do you understand, sir? You can visit us and try anything on at any time, and you don't have to buy anything if you don't want to. Please sit back and relax. Our shop is here for you. We can help you, but only if you want us to."*

If you have ever taken a tight shoe off, you can understand the relief I experienced after that short speech in my own language. I relaxed. Of course, I did end up buying shoes in that shop. More importantly, I was so impressed with their care for me that I brought many other customers to that shop!

Advice № 9
Price and Value

Value consists of the benefits that the customer is aware of and cares about. Price will impact the customer's desire to save money. This is the heart of the purchase process, as well as the sales process. You need to understand this in order to manage this process effectively, and not fall victim to the average salesman's most common complaint: "The customer went with the competitor to get a lower price."

Please note the customer does not purchase based on the "Price" alone, he purchases the *perceived profit,* which is the *positive* difference between Price and Value.

It's very easy to see that Price becomes most important *only* when the customer doesn't see or understand all the benefits. This happens because the sales rep doesn't make sure the customer has seen and understood all the benefits (Value). When the Value is completely understood by the customer, the Price becomes less important in the buying decision.

Your willingness to understand this data is the key factor in your success. Once you truly understand this fact, you will be consistently able to influence the customer's decision in a positive manner. If you don't understand this concept, you will end up arguing about the price, and the customer's attention will go to the competition and their potentially lower price.

Rule:

- *The customer buys the Profit not the PRICE! (Profit = Value minus Price)*
- *The Profit is a positive difference between Price and Value; Profit only becomes visible when the sales rep directs the customer's attention to the Value – the Price is normally obvious to the customer.*
- *The Value consists of all the benefits, and there can be a large number of benefits.*
- *The goal of any sales rep is to get the customer talking and*

discover the factors which can be turned into benefits for that specific customer, and then show as many benefits to the customer as possible.

- *The ability to handle the customer's unwillingness to look at the benefits of the product or service and to get the customer talking about them, as well as the ability to hold the customer's attention on these things during the whole process of selling, is one of the most important abilities of a sales rep.*

You always know if you are doing your job right or not. It's easy for everyone to see.

If you ask the customer questions about the benefits of the product or service, and you get the customer talking about how these benefits improve his life, you are doing your job right, you and the customer will be having more fun and your closing rate will increase as a result.

If you find you are arguing with the customer about the price and negative factors of your product or service, you are not only wasting your valuable time and upsetting potential customers, you are also sabotaging your own success.

Advice № 10
What do People Really Buy?

People do not buy goods or services. They do not buy "things." People buy because of their emotions. They buy based on what they "feel" about the product or service. They feel "bad" or "good" and that results in either a sale or just walking away. And this emotion is created out of the discussion of the benefits, which they can fully understand, and in turn relate to others, which results in "referral sales."

Whoever shows the most benefits wins!

The real secret of product benefits:

The same benefit, acts like a <u>new</u> and <u>separate</u> benefit <u>every time</u> it is brought to the customer's attention! The customer's interest in the product increases every time <u>either</u> the sales rep <u>or</u> the customer talks about any particular benefit. Each time a benefit is brought up in conversation, it increases the positive emotion and willingness of the customer to buy your product.

The main goal in sales is to help people create POSITIVE FEELINGS regarding the products they are looking to buy. This is a huge addition to the material benefit of the purchase and is very often worth more than money. The product sitting there silently or the price tag can't create these positive emotions. Advertising on the internet will try to do this, and can help to start the process, but it can only actually be done by a good sales rep asking the right questions and LISTENING to the customer!

Advice № 11
What Motivates People?

Logical explanations may get some people to think.

EMOTION makes people ACT!

How do you create the right emotion to get someone to ACT? Emotions are part of any experience, good or bad.

EMOTIONS create the action needed to <u>avoid</u> something <u>bad</u> or <u>acquire</u> something <u>good</u>.

There is a way to create the right emotions: <u>you</u> get the customer to think about certain situations in his life.

How?

Ask him about past situations with negative emotions in his life and then show how your product will help him avoid similar negative emotions in the future. Ask him about positive situations in the past and then show how your product can help him achieve those positive emotions again!

From this we can derive the main competitive advantage of the best sales professionals:

They know that having a lower price or a better product does NOT guarantee the sale!

They know that having the ability to **ignite** the **benefits** in the mind of the customer, creating positive ideas and emotions about their product guarantees a much, much higher closing rate.

To achieve this the sales rep must find and <u>practice</u> ways to smoothly discuss the benefits with the customer not just one time, but many times, asking the customer about his experiences and then always steering the customer back to the benefits at every opportunity.

How do you use this to the best advantage for both you and the customer? You should be interested in the customer's needs and experiences, find what emotions match those experiences, and continue to ask more questions. You will find people LOVE to talk about themselves, so give them the opportunity to do that! It's easy... Just ask them to tell you about their life experiences, especially as related to your product. They will talk about things that are interesting to them. And you will help customers close themselves on your product, IF you just give them a chance to talk before, during and after you point out the benefits.

Advice № 12
Customer Viewpoint on Quality

What is "quality" from the viewpoint of the customer? Simply put, how does the customer decide if your product is bad or good?

The perception of quality of products or services is based on the degree of satisfying the customer's *expectations*.

Did they get what they expected? Did they get exactly what they wanted? Did they get what they were promised by you? Any product has to "look good" to the customer at the time they buy it, but it also has to perform some useful function for the person after they get home. The suit fits perfectly in the store, but it should continue to fit perfectly for a long time after; it should be easy to clean and look good when it's pulled out of the suitcase on a business trip. The same story holds true with furniture. This is true for any product or service. It should continue to provide good value to the customer after he uses it for a while. What does "good value" mean for your customer in the long run? How do you prevent complaints or returns?

A tremendous amount of complaints and dissatisfaction occur for two main reasons:

1. The sales rep didn't find out what value the customer expected from using the product or service.

2. The sales rep promised more benefits than the product or service actually delivers.

What are the future features or benefits this particular customer expects when he uses it? This becomes the exact reason many sales aren't made in the first place! The customer can't trust a sales rep who doesn't show that he cares about how the customer is going to use the product or service in the future, and doesn't take the time to really find out what the customer expects from that product or service.

Advice № 13
Financial Advisor

A Financial Advisor is a person you are willing to take important advice from; such as, "How should I invest my hard earned savings?" This is a "trusted" person that people feel comfortable asking for advice when they are in doubt about a financial service or product.

As a result of many surveys, we found that a great Financial Advisor has 4 main qualities from the <u>customer's</u> viewpoint:

1. *This person is on **my** side. He is interested in **my** future benefit.*
2. *This person is an expert in the subject being discussed.*
3. *This person finds out exactly what **my** problems are and he understands what **I** need.*
4. *He will not force me to make a fast decision; he will make sure I have the information I need, and he will allow me to decide for myself and make the best choice for me.*

If a customer feels that the sales rep has these qualities above, then at the moment of making a decision, the customer will listen to his advice. If not, the customer will NOT listen to the sales rep, but will go off to *think* about it.

Here is the main point:

These valuable qualities only exist if the sales rep concentrates on benefits for the customer. The benefits will become obvious when the customer begins to use what he bought. If the sales rep wants to make sure that the customer will be happy with the results of using that product or service, he will take an interest in the future value while talking with his customer.

And the problem of "What questions should I ask to find out what the customer really wants?" will not exist. This problem only exists when a sales rep actually just wants to ask: "Well, are you going to buy this or not?" or "When are you going to pay?" This is not the champion's attitude, and it results in uncomfortable silence or meaningless chatter, and a dissatisfied customer.

Anybody will answer questions about topics that they find interesting. It's much easier to show the true qualities of a product or service when you get the customer talking about what interests him, and if you show that you are truly interested in the customer's future benefit. Champions realize quickly when the customer is not interested in the sales pitch, and they immediately start asking questions to find out what the customer is interested in. Interestingly, customers are never interested in the sales rep's problems or commission.

True product quality and value becomes visible <u>only</u> in use. The proof of a good sales rep is a Low Complaint Percentage and a High Referral Rate after the sale. The sales rep must always understand the true long-term quality of his product or service in order to direct the customer's attention to the long-term benefits. When this is done correctly, there is no question of selling your product or service at a discount or arguing over price.

One of the traps for unsuccessful sales reps is using language that confuses the customer. The best sales reps know the exact features and benefits of their products or services. The very best sales reps know the list of positive characteristics and everything that makes up the "value" for the customer and they always describe these characteristics in words the customer can easily understand.

The customer's language is the language of benefits, advantages and long-term value. The product's language is made up of technical features, with technical words describing those features. Customers tend to get confused by all the technical language used to describe the product. Remember your last trip to a doctor? They use fancy Latin words to tell you what is wrong with you. This results in confusion about your condition, a very uncomfortable feeling and the result is: who likes to go to a doctor?

The sales rep is the translator! He is expected to fully understand technical product language and turn around and explain the technical features of the product in simple words that show the benefit to the customer. The words "good," "best" or "interesting" will communicate nothing to a customer regarding the value of the product. These general opinions irritate customers and reduce their trust in the sales rep.

The proper viewpoint:
"How can I help my customer see and fully understand the value and future benefits of this product?"

This means the best sales reps fully understand the technical features and how to describe those features in simple terms that show the true benefit to the customer. This results in a customer who understands what the product or service is going to do to make his life better, and when he gets home, the product or service should meet or exceed his expectations.

This is vitally important, and Champions know that this alone is what sets them above their peers. Champions do NOT over promise and under deliver. Champions fully understand the value of their product and simply communicate that value to their customer. Champions fully expect their customer to be able to explain the value they received to others, which results in referral sales. Champions fully expect their customers to be very satisfied with the product after they get home and use it!

Advice № 15
Professionalism

Regarding sales, there are three abilities that distinguish professionals from amateurs:

1. The skill of asking proper questions.

2. The skill of really listening to a customer, not interrupting him and not finishing his sentences or thoughts when he pauses to think.

3. The skill to utilize the customer's answers to explain simply and honestly how the product will benefit the customer in the long-term.

Advice № 16
Dreams and Goals

If you are able to dream up a goal, you are able to achieve it.

There is no goal you can dream of, that you can't achieve. But any dream will require you to take action to make it become reality. The size of your dream will determine how many actions you will have to take to achieve it. Every person can achieve their dream IF they are willing to do all the actions necessary.

Are you willing to do what is necessary to achieve the goals you dream of?

The bigger your goals, the more actions you must be willing to take and continue as long as necessary to reach your goals and fulfill your dream.

You can achieve any goal that you can dream up, but only if you are willing to roll up your sleeves and persist in correct actions that move you closer and closer to your goal.

Advice № 17
How to become a Winner

Who becomes a Winner in this world?

Anyone who is willing to take more action, complete more effective steps, talk to more people and persist as long as it takes to reach the goal they dream up.

The conclusion is very simple:

You will win:

if you act and act and act and never quit taking effective actions that move you in the direction of your goal. Maybe you already know this. Maybe you think only the quality of your action is important. But, very often the reason for failure in any activity is simply *not enough* action taken, no matter how great the product or service is.

There's an old saying, "the world will beat a path to buy a better mousetrap."

That's not true.

There are countless businesses and sales reps that have failed because they were "waiting" for people to come and buy their high quality products.

To be truly successful, you must have a good quality product or service. But, if you spend most of your time trying to make it perfect and too little time and action letting people know you have a good product, you will fail.

The truth is simple.

If you are willing to spend enough time and effective action letting everyone know you have a good product, you will win.

Advice № 18
Opinion Trap

A person usually starts doing a new activity with desire and enthusiasm.

Would you agree that their beginning steps are normally less than perfect?

This is the moment when "opinions" start trapping people. There are many opinions. "Was it done with high quality and attention to detail?"
"Was enough time spent preparing the product?"
"Was enough training done first?"

There seem to be many "expert" opinions on what is right and what is wrong. Some will say don't even start selling until your product or service is perfect.

As a rule, those who never achieve success are too busy "perfecting" the product to satisfy other peoples' opinions. They never get out and talk to enough potential customers every single day.

Winners continually work to upgrade their knowledge, their skill and their product or service. BUT they never use that as a reason for not talking to more people than any of their competitors or co-workers.

This assumes you have a good, workable product or service that delivers what you promise. The emphasis is on workable!

When you start to do anything,
It's like you're writing on blank wall.
The tiniest mistake you make will stick out for all to see.
Those who do nothing, write nothing on the wall,
And they are always the worst critics of your "mistakes."
But, the critic never gets anything done either.
So beware the trap of another's "helpful" opinion.

A statement by Michael Jordan, one of the most successful basketball players of all-time, illustrates this phenomenon very well:

"Throughout my entire career, I missed over 9000 shots and I lost over 300 games. 29 times I was trusted to take the last shot so that my team could win, and I missed. I lost again and again, but I kept playing, that's why I'm a champion!"

Advice № 19
Fear of Error

The most dangerous trap is listening to everyone's opinions on quality and perfection, and worrying about what someone else is going to say about your delivery or your product. This is especially difficult when there are many "clever" critics around. Their slogan is "Prove you're the best, then maybe I'll buy."

If you constantly try to prove yourself to others, you fall into a horrible trap. It will stop you and kill your dreams, unless you are fully aware of this trap.

If you focus all your efforts on avoiding failure and mistakes, or you fear looking like an idiot, you will lose. You may even forget your dreams and goals entirely and wander off looking for an "easier" job.

We're not just talking about the external critics (customers and co-workers and managers) we're also talking about "you" criticizing you (internal criticism). Sometimes you can be your own worst enemy. This external and internal criticism can destroy your most important ability: the ability to take action and to take joy and pleasure in your own motion.

Fear of failure attracts failure like a magnet. What you are afraid of, you will get.

Focus on the truth.

The truth is, right at this moment, you are able to take some action and get things done.

The more actions you take, the more good results you achieve. The more good results you achieve, the better and more professional you become. The more professional you are, the more successful you become.

Winners are made... not born.

Winners are not afraid to make mistakes.

Winners are busy doing something effective, not sitting around and criticizing the efforts of others.

Jim's first sales experience:

I showed up at the meeting place for my first door-to-door sales experience. I was a professional nuclear engineer and I was ready for a new career and the opportunity to make a lot more money. I was eager to learn and excited to meet the team. My friend told me he made a ton of money every weekend. I believed him.

I wore my nicest golf shorts and golf shirt. The Training Manager was late, so I had time to ask the dozen sales reps standing around about their experience with this awesome sales opportunity. The first guy looked at me and said: *"You can't make sales in shorts!"* I was a little dismayed, but I reminded myself that my friend made a lot of money. I asked how many sales I could expect to make on my first day. Everyone laughed and said zero! At that moment the Trainer walked in and started handing out area assignments. I was thinking I made a big mistake, and I just gave up a beautiful golf day just to waste my time. As I was starting to slide out the door to escape, the Trainer grabbed me and said: *"let's go!"*

By this time, my initial enthusiasm was dashed, but I had promised my friend I would try it out, and I really needed to increase my income. The Trainer walked up to the first house, knocked on the door, explained the benefit of the discount card, collected the money and we walked away. It happened so fast, I wasn't even sure of what he said to the customer. The product was a discount card for a local car repair shop. It really was a no-brainer. The cost was $20 and the customer got 3 free oil changes worth $45, plus another $500 of discounts on car repairs. I was ready to buy one myself.

After he sold five customers in a row, I told him to give me the discount card so I could sell the next customer. This was too easy! He was so comfortable talking the customers and explaining the benefits and answering their questions, and collecting $20 bills. He told me to wait. He said he had to show me how to handle an objection. The very next guy was very serious and antagonistic and wouldn't look or listen, no matter what the Trainer said. After 10 minutes, the Trainer gave up and we walked away.

I said: *"You mean some people won't listen no matter what you say? Give me the discount card!"*

I knocked on the next door and a 16 year old boy answered. My first thought was to ask for his parents. My next thought was to practice my first pitch on this young guy. I started to show him the card and the discounts and the other benefits. He started laughing and pointed to his "new" car in the driveway and said he needed every service on the card (his "new" car was 20 years old). He asked me to wait a minute while he grabbed some money. He came back with $40 and said his best friend had a "new" car too. I made a double commission on my very first sale.

I made mistakes that first day, but the Trainer was there to help me out and I listened to his advice eagerly and I made 20 sales that day not zero!

Important Rule:
Sell something you like, only take advice from a Professional, ignore negative and critical people, and go into action.

I've been a salesman ever since that day and I never stop learning how to be more professional.

Advice № 20
Who is More Alive?

There are those who try to do something new without any errors or failures. They try to bypass problems completely and they end up losing time and money and pride. But if they never study or attempt something new, then they really aren't really living life at all. They aren't participating in life, they act like spectators watching a "movie" about life, and they aren't even one of the actors in the movie.

There's an old story; a rich person was asked how he became "rich." As any active and successful person would be, his answer was quick and straight to the point:

- "Two words," he said.
- "Yes?"
- "Right actions."
- "And before that?"
- "Wide experience."
- "And before that?"
- "Wrong actions."

You want to start living?

Get very busy.
Get very active.
Don't be afraid to make some mistakes.
Learn from your mistakes and then get even busier.
You will definitely feel more Alive!

If you do that, you will succeed.

Advice № 21
Thinking about Failure Can Stop You

To fully understand how thinking about potential failure can cut down your willingness to act in a certain area, let's look at two types of response to your proposal.

First type:
You tell people about your product. They not only refuse to buy from you, but also make antagonistic remarks about you, your information or your product. They are not happy that you showed up at all, and they make that very clear to you.

How willing are you to keep talking with these customers?

Second type:
You tell people about your product. They don't always buy your product, but they're always glad to see you, they think your product information is very interesting and they make positive remarks about your proposal even if they don't buy right then.

How willing are you to keep talking with these customers?

Think about this for a moment.

Which type of customer are you willing to be more persistent with? Which type of customer do you think you will be happy and successful with?

Here is the main secret: *people's attitude toward you, your presence and your proposals, will depend on **you** only.*

*You can **always** positively influence the customer's attitude.* Learn this secret and you will always be successful and you will become a Champion.

Jim's experience in Virginia:

I was running a door-to-door sales crew one night in northern Virginia. There were some "old-timers" and some brand new sales reps. I was handing out maps of the territories each rep was to work that night, and one of the old-timers pointed at one map and said that neighborhood was terrible. Another experienced rep agreed and said nobody ever bought anything from anyone in that crummy neighborhood. I took this as a challenge to prove the point above. I informed all the reps that there were no bad neighborhoods and I took the map for that area and challenged everyone that I would take the worst neighborhood and make twice as many sales as they would. Three hours later, we met back up, and I had made a dozen sales. They shook their heads in disbelief. Nobody else had more than six sales. My positive attitude "infected" the crummy neighborhood, and I talked to a lot of interesting people, they didn't all buy from me, but everyone was nice to me.

Advice № 22
Action is Senior

Here's another trap: you stop taking action because somebody else thinks that what you are doing or saying is wrong.

This is the trap: you stop and "think" instead of just going into action.

How often does this occur in sales?

Every day.

For example:

- Sales reps won't approach those customers who don't look "friendly."
- Sales reps think it's "rude" to ask a lot of "personal" questions.
- It's not generally accepted to take an active interest in the customers' problems.
- It's too hard to direct the customer's attention back to the benefits already discussed.
- If the customer says, "I need to think about it." The sales rep thinks the sale is over.

These are "bad" ideas for sales reps to "believe." They stop to "think" about the problems instead of going into action and communication. They stop trying.

A Champion is willing and able to easily make any sales proposal, to anyone he chooses. He doesn't stop to "think" any negative thoughts about anyone, he just goes into action, and he confidently controls his own attitude and he communicates effectively with any customer.

Advice № 23
The Principle of a Champion

A Champion never has the feeling he "must close" every single prospect. The principle of a Champion is very simple:

The Champion *invests himself in everyone he meets, without "counting on" any one prospect. This is the key. He knows he can change anyone's attitude positively, whether he closes them or not.*

He is not afraid to "lose" a prospect! He makes a huge number of proposals to many prospects. He doesn't carefully choose the "good" or "happy" prospects. He doesn't spend a lot of time thinking or worrying, "Should I tell this person about my products or not?" He just goes ahead with no fear or worry, and confidently offers his product to a tremendous number of people!

He never fears losing a specific prospect. He never allows himself to get into a situation where he has a "shortage" of prospects. He always ensures he has an unlimited supply of prospects.

Andrey's experience in London:
Years ago, I walked by a top quality men's clothing store. Beautiful suits were displayed in the shop window. The prices were very high, even for London. The quality caught my attention and I stopped. The prices were way out of my league, but I was interested enough to walk in and take a closer look. I was very alert and cautious. The salesman in the back of the store noticed me. He gave me time to look around and then greeted me: *"Hello! I am here to help you, if you need me."* I was afraid he would try to pressure me to buy something and I quickly told him: *"I'm just looking."*

He said: *"I understand. Let's make a deal right now."*

"What kind of deal? I am not buying anything!" I replied tensely.

He confidently stated: *"That's fine. Let's make a deal that you are <u>not</u> buying anything from me now. You just look around. Let me* *explain why our shop is different from the others and why our prices are higher, and we both agree you* **can't buy** *anything during this visit. If you decide to come back another time, I'll be more than glad to help you choose something you like. If you don't come back, that's okay too. Deal?"*

I agreed to that "deal" and I stayed. I relaxed. Here was a sales professional rich in prospects, and he was totally confident of the quality and value of his products. He wasn't the owner, but he was proud of their high prices and he was not trying to talk me into buying anything. He didn't push me away. He treated me with respect and said "no" to me before I could say "no" to him.

He toured me around the shop. He explained the purpose and philosophy of the owners, where the clothes came from and how they were made. I was listening to him and many things became clear to me. The prices didn't seem as high as they did when I first walked in. He asked what I was interested in and I said I wanted to buy a beautiful tie that caught my eye as he was talking.

He said: *"Great. It was a pleasure to talk with you. And now, have a nice evening."*

"Wait a minute. I want to buy this tie."

He smiled and reminded me: *"We made a deal when you walked in. You promised not to buy anything now."*

I really wanted to buy that tie, so I said: *"Nice joke. I'm serious, I really want to buy that tie."*

He said calmly: *"It wasn't a joke. I meant it. I didn't do this to trick you into buying something now. Many people leave and come back later to buy something."*

I had to go out the front door and then walk back in again to buy that tie, which I still own and use today!

Advice № 24
What Champions Pay Attention To

Champions know exactly what to pay attention to.

This is what makes them the best.

No matter what you sell, there is always a common denominator of any sale. You always sell exactly one thing. Always, no matter what else is going on.

Whatever the result of the meeting, the main thing you have to sell is the next meeting or contact. This is important.

Professionals know that the next meeting is much, much, much more important than just getting paid right now!

Get that next meeting lined up, even if it's a follow-up call after the close.

The more prospects you talk to... the more loyal customers you will create.

Advice № 25
Strong Positioning

Wealthy people and companies always build and maintain a strong "position" in the mind of their customers. "Positioning" is the idea that distinguishes the company or rep from all the others. Smart companies and reps know exactly what quality distinguishes them from all the rest. They never have to "prove" they are the best. Their attitude reflects supreme confidence in their company, their product and their own ability. This is a very important rule in achieving success and wealth.

To ensure success, you should always be first and foremost in the minds of those who use your products or service.

You should be different from everyone else! That's how you position yourself. You give the customer reasons to remember you above all others. Your attitude, your professionalism, your product knowledge, your willingness to let the customers talk about themselves - these all lead to a strong "position" in the customer's mind.

Wealthy and successful people always know their own value, the value of their company and the value of their products relative to other sales reps and companies.

The Champion is always confident about this fact and never tries to prove anything to anybody. "I know who I am, what I'm selling and I'm proud of my company." A Champion always makes sure he is representing the best product or service.

He confidently leads the customer through all the hurdles to a full understanding of his product or service.

Trying to prove or persuade equals "justifying some hidden weakness" to a customer. And this is an indicator of a poor salesman.

Advice № 26
Have You Been Taught to Pretend?

Have you been taught to sell by learning to say or do things that you would never do naturally?

Have you been taught to just memorize a script and pretend to be someone or something you are not?

If so, you will find yourself under continual stress at your job. You will never earn a lot of money if you are constantly stressed out!

Rule:
> *Be yourself! Learn to talk to people pleasantly, naturally, like you do with your friends, and then apply that same natural communication in sales. You and your customers will have more fun communicating with each other.*
> *Learn to communicate easily and watch your commissions multiply!*

Older sales schools had a passion for "tricks" and unusual solutions for getting customers to say "yes" whether they really wanted the product or not. These "tricks" have given the honorable profession of sales a bad name and have left a sour taste in the mouth of many customers. These tricks were born from a misunderstanding of the basic truths of sales.

Like any profession, there are basic truths that are very simple to learn and lead to consistent results. If you understand them, and **practice** them honestly, you will become a very competent sales professional. If you continue to practice and improve, you will become a sales Champion.

The sales profession is one of the highest paid professions in the world! But why is it that 20% of the sales reps make 80% of the sales?

Because 80% of all sales reps tend to complicate the whole process, and end up with bad results, upset customers, a lot of stress, and too little commission. The "lucky" ones seem to always be at the top of the commission scale.

It's not luck.

The best sales professionals truly understand, practice and apply the basic principles of sales consistently. When these basic truths are known and applied, it looks like magic. Anyone can learn the basics and become a professional, and with enough practice, a Champion.

How do Champion sports teams continue to be Champions? Is it just luck? Is it just money? NO! They practice the fundamentals over and over, day after day. Professional athletes spend much more time practicing than they do actually playing the game.

Do you want to be a Champion? Be honest with yourself.

If your answer is yes, then you must decide to practice your professional skills until they are easy to do. With practice, these fundamental truths become part of your normal daily actions. You will start to apply the basic principles without having to stop and think about what to do or say to help the customer make a choice, and close the deal.

And the best part is, if you are willing to practice and become a Champion, you and your customer are happy and you BOTH WIN. No stress, no strain, for you or the customer, and you help the customer achieve what he wants and you make MUCH higher commissions consistently.

These basic truths apply to any type of sale; on the phone, face to face, door to door, residential, small business, retail business, commercial, industrial, corporate or government. The basic principles never change.

If you fully understand something and you practice it until you can do it in your sleep, you will consistently achieve the results you desire, and ultimately, you will achieve any goal you can dream up financially.

Rule:

The Champion always behaves the same way with the customer as he does in the rest of his life. He never has to pretend, he knows what to say and do. And he learns this by practicing the art of sales every day.

When talking with any customer, he communicates the same way as he does with his friends, naturally, easily and pleasantly. That's why he can do his job without stress.

Advice № 27
Why Salesmen Stop Liking their Products

During our case studies, we consistently observed the following action:

At the end of the proposal or pitch, the sales rep asks the customer if he is going to buy the product. If the customer says "no," the rep tends to ask the customer what he *doesn't* like about the product. Instantly, all the customer's attention goes on the drawbacks, not the advantages.

Sales rep: *"Will that be cash or credit?"*
Customer: *"We're going to look for something else. This isn't exactly what we wanted."*
Sales rep: *"What didn't you like?"*

And they start talking about "what the customer didn't like."
Size, shape, color, price, etc.

What happens?
If only 2 out of 10 customers were closed – and unfortunately this is the average around the world – the sales rep has "listened" to 80% of the prospects complaining about the product's drawbacks. Now, by the end of day, the sales rep becomes totally convinced that there are many more drawbacks to his product than advantages. In other words, the customer has "sold" the sales rep.

Unless YOU want to be convinced by your prospects all day, every day, that your product or service is not worth paying for, YOU must change something immediately!

FIRST, make sure you fully understand all the advantages of your product or service. If you have honestly found out everything about what you are being paid to sell, and you realize you would not buy this product or service for your own family or friends, then go find a better product or service to sell. If you realize after close observation that your product or service is truly valuable for people you actually care about, then study all the reasons why you should sell your product or service, and memorize these benefits! True Champions never sell anything they don't believe in.

QUIT asking what they didn't like or why they didn't buy. Remember, the customer always has the right "To buy or not to buy." You have the right to find out what the customer *did* like about your product!

START asking questions about what they like about your product and also remind them about all the attributes of your product, and get them telling you the effect those attributes will have on their life.

Advice № 28
What Wealthy People Always Have

Wealthy people always have things they enjoy, things that bring them pleasure. And normally, they are willing to share the things they enjoy. The have beautiful houses and throw big parties to share their wealth with their friends. They have nice cars and boats and invite their friends to enjoy them as well. They have planes and invite their friends to fly with them.

Poor people always have things they **don't** like, things they love to complain about. And the things they do like always seem to belong to someone else. They are always looking over there, never enjoying what they actually own. It doesn't mean they have no money. It just means they have a "poor" attitude toward life and material objects.

The viewpoint of a wealthy person: *"I enjoy what I have, and I'm always willing to share."*

The viewpoint of a poor person: *"I don't have anything I like, I wish I had what they have."*

Wealthy thought: *"I always HAVE something valuable."*

Poor thought: *"I NEVER have anything valuable."*

Hence the rule of success:

Always love what you have and be willing to share this with others. For a Champion it's a guiding rule. Champions focus on the positive in everything they do and have, and they are constantly trying to share this positive attitude with everyone they meet.

Advice № 29
Which Quality are You "Rich" with?

Everybody gives something to the people around him:
words, thoughts, actions, looks and emotions.
These can be perceived by anyone.

A definite trace of this "gift" stays with a customer after you talk with them.

And the secret is, people always give something they consider they have a large amount of.

People give to others what they believe they are "rich" in,
something they have naturally accumulated their whole life.

If you accumulated joy, then you will give out joy. If you accumulated a lot of kindness and love toward people, you will leave kindness and love behind with everyone you talk to. If you accumulated spite or fear, then you will hand out spite and fear to everyone you meet.

People who are chronically afraid, leave fear behind them.

If you are full of respect toward yourself, then it is much easier to give respect and support to others.

If you don't appreciate yourself, it is much harder to appreciate others.

A true winner treats others as winners.

In sales, this mechanism displays itself very clearly because the following law is always in play: "Before you take, you must give."

And what do the best sales reps normally give?
Something they think will have *value* when it is given.

That's why it's very important for a sales rep to think well of himself, his product and his company. Anyone can change how they think about themselves, their product and their company, if they really want to.

What "gift" are you giving your customers? It may take some work and practice to improve your gift, but aren't you worth it?

Is achieving your goals worth your effort and dedication to improve the way you think about yourself, your product and your company?

When you are confident in yourself, your customers can see that. And, when they can see you truly believe in your product and you genuinely want to assist them in choosing the product and living life better for it, you move from being "someone who wants to sell something" to a "friendly advisor." When you deliver a product worth having, you get more referrals and repeat sales.

Advice № 30
Hard Work Trap

A definition of *Hard Work*:
Doing something you don't enjoy, so you can make enough money to barely survive today and take a vacation some time in the future, maybe.

Don't fall into the "hard work" trap! If you already have, get out of it!

"I'll do this job just a little longer, and *then* I will start to enjoy my life."

Some people live their whole life working with this idea in mind. This only occurs because a person doesn't love his job and he's just waiting for that happy moment when the hard work will all be over. The money keeps them going back to the same old grind. But money doesn't have much meaning if a person gets no pleasure from making it.

Here is what Mark Twain said on this subject:

"The law of work does seem utterly unfair - but there it is, and nothing can change it: the higher the pay in enjoyment the worker gets out of it, the higher shall be his pay in cash, too." From "A Connecticut Yankee In King Arthur's court."

"He would have comprehended that Work consists of whatever a body is OBLIGED to do, and that Play consists of whatever a body is not obliged to do. And this would help him to understand why constructing artificial flowers or performing on a tread-mill is work, while rolling ten-pins or climbing Mont Blanc is only amusement." From "The Adventures of Tom Sawyer."

You can very quickly start to hate your job if you forget why you liked it in the first place and you start thinking only about the money you get from it.

Jim's experience:

After I got out of the Navy, I was working for the U.S. government Trident Submarine new construction. I hated my job. I hated getting out of bed in the morning. I walked slowly to my office every day. I was getting numb.

One day a friend told me he was making $1000 a weekend in door-to-door sales. It seemed unbelievable at first, but I was getting desperate about my future. I was nearing 30 and I didn't want to be stuck in a job I hated for the rest of my life. He convinced me to try it. I went out my first Saturday, learned the ropes, loved the product myself and I made $50/hour. That was *twice as much money* as I made as a professional, licensed nuclear engineer with nearly 7 years of college and post-graduate education. Unbelievable! The best part was that I had fun talking to people, and the four hours flew by like a warm summer breeze.

I made myself a promise. I would only sell things I would gladly offer to my 85 year-old grandmother. If something was good enough for me and my family to use, then I would sell it to others. That has been my guiding principle for over 25 years.

The funny part was my mom was very upset that I quit my nice, safe, secure, boring government job to be a door-to-door salesman. I told her that I wanted a job that I could have fun doing every day. Her words to me were: *"Oh, honey, work is not fun, it's something hard that you have to do to take care of your family and you can have fun when you retire."* I love my mom. Years later, when she saw that I was a successful business owner, happily married and gave her two grandsons, she admitted that maybe you could have a high paying job that was fun too.

Advice № 31
The Fundamental Law Of Success

When you do something you love to do, you will find it's easy to do and takes very little effort. You can't be stopped by anything or anyone when you are doing something you love to do. This is the fundamental law of success: the more actions you complete in a workday, the more successful you are. The more you love your work, the more actions you are willing to complete.

Do more, think less.

Actions completed lead to success.

Of course you need knowledge to succeed, but it will come more readily to those who are willing to act, not to those who are sitting around, thinking about their problems.

Knowledge will bring nothing to those who are doing nothing. Never try to teach an idler, especially one, who claims they never make a mistake. They never make mistakes, because they never do anything. Your knowledge will be wasted if you try to share it with someone who is unwilling to take action.

Law of success:
If you love what you are doing, you will be willing to complete a lot of actions every day. You will do these actions frequently, you will not stop doing these actions, you will be called "lucky" and you will make much more money easily.

Advice № 32
Follow Your Passion

Those who do their work with great pleasure will be paid more.

Look... would you like to pay your money to a sales rep who stands in front of you with a dull face and shows that he is bored to death with both you and this job, and he would be happy to leave it all right now if he could? Have you ever been to a restaurant where the waiters don't want to do their jobs? They don't like their profession, they don't like their restaurant and they don't like their customers. It's obvious to anyone who walks in the door. Unfortunately there are too many similar examples because it occurs way too often.

Can you think of some positive examples you experienced recently? Have you been helped by someone who loved their job. They were happy you walked in so they could help you? Did you notice how this attracted your attention? Can you think of the last time you actually thanked a sales rep as you paid them for the product or service? Isn't it much nicer to walk away from a sales transaction with a smile on your face and spring in your step?

Love and pleasure from what you do directly influences your ability to have a lot of money without being stressed out.

Many people say this concept is too simple.

Luckily for you, it is very simple. This is the whole trick.

Observe for yourself. Look at the "lucky" ones.

What do they have in common?

They love what they're doing all day long.
They can't wait to get to work in the morning.
They are the last to leave the office.
They love their company.
They love their product or service.

They have closed contracts waiting for them on Monday morning.

They really are "lucky."

Advice № 33
Two Main Qualities

There are two main qualities or skills of a professional sales rep, and the rest of the necessary skills follow them:

The First Quality: *total certainty* of the ability to do one's job under any circumstances, with any customer, in any situation, no matter how uncomfortable.

If you already have this quality, then everything else you learn in this book will help you become a very wealthy Sales Champion.

If you don't have this quality already, don't give up, you can acquire this quality by practicing the advices of this book every day, until you notice that all of a sudden, you do have total certainty of your ability.

The Second Quality: the *willingness and skill to find solutions that really work for different situations,* knowing and using the fundamental laws.

The fundamental laws of professional salesmanship are in this book. It's impossible to give you specific advice for every single situation you could run into in your career. There are an unlimited number of completely different situations you could face. Our purpose is to teach you to find your own words, your own pitch, and your own solutions to handle any situation you run into. If your willingness to find solutions is based on the proper *fundamental laws*, you will be very successful, stress-free, super confident and very highly paid.

Champions become Champions because they understand and apply the basic fundamental laws to their profession.

Champions aren't just born that way, they study, practice and learn to be Champions and so can you.

Advice № 34
The Essence of Buying

When we go to buy anything, what do we do?

Which words best describe the essence of this daily process? Usually, it's words like "choose," "look for," "select" or "decide."

If we go to the store, what should we be able to do? We should be able to properly and quickly choose what we need and want.

The essence of buying is *choice*. Making the best choice out of a seemingly huge number of options. There can be a lot of stress involved in making the right choice.

When we buy something, we have to "choose" something we want or need.

Why do you ask your friend for advice before you buy? He already owns the thing you want to buy. What are you going to do with his advice? You are hoping for good information that you TRUST so you can make the right choice, which will be the best choice for you and your situation.

This is exactly what you should always remember when you sell anything.

The essence of your job is:
Help the customer to choose the best option for the <u>customer</u>!

Advice № 35
What Do You Offer?

You are basically offering information as a service to the customer. You are not offering the product. You are there to offer information as a service in order to help the customer make the best choice as quickly and efficiently as possible.

The product once sold can then be handled or delivered by other people. If the salesman handles or delivers the product himself, it is treated as a separate action from the process of the actual sale *(sale = helping the customer make the best possible choice)*.

The process of any sale is often confused with: "offering" a product and telling the customer to buy it. When you don't give the information necessary to make a good decision and allow the customer the right to choose, you get a very complicated subject called *sales*! This complicated subject requires a lot of advice and "authoritative" opinions on how to "manipulate" and "shove" and "pressure" and "trick" customers into "buying" a product so the company can profit and the sales rep can make enough money to barely survive.

As a result, we have a public image of a manipulative "salesman" which is widely spread around the world: smooth, fast talking, high pressure, dishonest, and persistently annoying enough to make people do what they don't want to do: to buy something they really didn't want to buy.

Sometimes it appears that the "best" sales reps master the "skills" above. But actually, Champions never sell this way, and they don't advise others to do it either. Those who teach manipulative sales "skills" are actually not able to sell. They have a hard time telling the truth to anyone, including themselves.

Any salesman taught high-pressure, manipulation sales techniques, actually never deals directly with the customer himself, he's only dealing with the customer's protest against this sales "technique." This is the cause of high stress and the sense that the salesman is in a battle "against" the customer, like the "Cold War." As a result, we get the feeling that customers don't want to buy or in general just don't like to talk to sales reps. You have probably heard many salesmen say, "buyers are liars," as they walk away from another failed close.

Nothing mentioned above cancels the main qualities of a Champion – certainty and ability to complete a large number of actions. But this certainty and activity should be directed to giving the customer the right information to make the best choice, which actually creates their desire to purchase the product or service. If you press and squeeze the customer, *you* will be pressed and squeezed *by* the customer.

You get people interested in your product or service by being interested in them and their problems and then giving them the information they need, and earning their trust. The rest is easy, if you practice the principles outlined in this book.

Advice № 36
"I'll Think About It..."

Did you ever find yourself, as a customer, in a situation where you didn't really see the benefit of something and didn't choose to buy, but you didn't want to upset the sales rep. So you ask, "Are you are open tomorrow? How late? Will you be here then? Great! I just need more time to think about it." Wasn't that an attempt to leave without making the sales rep upset?

This excuse can dispirit any sales rep, decreasing the willingness to continue, and this is often the reason why people don't want to work in the sales area of most companies! The sales rep believes that the customer really did go to "think about" how he could buy it. But, he normally never comes back. Sound familiar to you?

Why does this happen? We want customers to buy now, not to "think about it and come back later."

Rule:
A Sales rep should gradually, step by step, create the decision to ACT in the customer's mind.

You can *use* any customer excuse, such as: "I'll think about it;" "We want to look at some other choices;" "I need to talk to my your spouse about it;" "We will come back later this afternoon;" in order to *continue* to talk with the potential customer.

Use their excuse to ask more questions.

Please note: don't use pressure, just continue to be interested in their problems and invite them to talk about their issues. Don't just quit after you hear, "I'll think about it." Don't push, but also don't let go.

Understand this! He isn't going away to "think," he's *just going away.*

Their actual excuse can help you rekindle their interest in your product:

"Yes, you should think about it. To make it easier for you, what is the benefit that you liked the most about this product? What problem are you trying to solve?"

These and other similar questions give you the chance to find out what else he needs to know about your product.

Advice № 37
The Best Advertising

Word of Mouth has always existed, and it will always continue to exist. It is based on the natural willingness of people to share their feelings (good or bad). We are not talking about media advertising designed to make some product well known. We mean that people, as a rule, love to tell others about things they like or dislike. Their opinion about a product or service can often be the decisive factor for the people who trust them, their friends and family.

Law:

Word of Mouth is the best advertising.

When your customer leaves you with the *unshakable certainty* that his decision to buy from you is absolutely correct, you can be sure that soon you'll have several new customers referred to you.

By taking the time and care to create this unshakeable certanty in you and your product, you are creating your future income!

By selling with the future in mind, you make it possible for the customer to make his own decision based on certainty, which is the result of trust, security and lack of doubt. The customer leaves knowing he can trust you, which means you must earn his trust in the beginning and maintain this trust throughout the sales process.

You should care about the customer, whether he buys something now or not, tell him something interesting about your product, find out what is important to him, and don't make a disgusted or disappointed face if he refuses to buy right now. You create trust with the customer by showing that you care more about his needs than your commission. Show him the benefits of your knowledge, your product, your company and you will create good will and a sense of trust. Do this, and then there is always the chance that either he himself or his friends or business partners will come back to you one more time. Keep creating the future and build trust, you will also feel better about yourself, your product and your company. Continue to do this with every prospect, and you will create a future filled with high pay and people that trust you and refer their friends and family to you.

Jim's story of the True Power of Word of Mouth:

I was selling dry cleaning discount cards door-to-door early one Saturday. The first house I came to belonged to an 87 year-old lady. I showed her the value of the discount cards and asked her about her family and friends. After a few minutes I realized that she didn't qualify to buy the card, as she really didn't do enough dry cleaning. I thanked her, wished her a good day and turned to run to the next house. She stopped me and said she wanted to buy one of the discount cards. I politely refused to sell her the card, because it would not benefit her, and I would feel bad about taking her money for nothing in exchange.

She insisted she wanted to buy, and I realized she wanted to give me something for being nice to her and listening to her stories of her grandchildren. I asked if she had any chocolate chip cookies. She laughed and invited me in for cookies and milk. I had already explained how the discount card worked, and she finally admitted she only took one blanket to be dry-cleaned every four years, and this meant that the discount card would last her for another 100 years! After a few minutes of friendly chatting and great cookies, I left, thanking her for the cookies and kindness.

As I approached the next house, the door opened before I could knock, and a young woman smiled and said, *"Hello Jim! I'll take two please!"*

I was shocked, and asked what she was talking about. She said she had a check made out already for two dry-cleaning discount cards.

The nice little old lady next door was very well known and loved in that neighborhood filled with young, urban, professional couples. She had called ahead and told everyone in the neighborhood that "Jim" was coming. She had memorized the sales pitch exactly, and told each person that they should buy two. I made over $1000 in commission in one day, a single day highest ever company sales record.

That is the power of Word of Mouth and an example of doing the right thing for the customer every time.

The other lesson here is: treat little old ladies with kindness and respect. They can be your best ally or your worst enemy. These days, they know how to use email, the internet and how to blog.

Disrespect your elders at your own risk.

Respect your elders and stand by for a lot of referrals.

Advice № 38
Your WORST Enemy

Your worst enemy is the customer's *doubt*. Not the price. There is a precise observation that proves that the more money someone pays, the more benefit they are able to get from any product or service.

Doubt, worry, uncertainty – they are the true enemy to every sales professional on the planet. And the weapon you use to handle it is <u>not</u> pressure or manipulation, but discussion of the *advantages* and *benefits* for the customer. Don't use all your "bullets" at once, but one by one. You don't even know yet what exact "enemies" you will have to handle. You don't know, because in the beginning of the sale, you have neither doubt nor interest. Doubts will appear in the form of "objections," then you will need your bullets – the benefits.

That's why you should start your pitch with the smaller advantages. Don't get yourself into the situation where the customer is almost ready to buy, and he gives you his last little doubt – which shows up in the form of an objection – and you have nothing left to say. Then you will feel pressure to make something up, and this usually irritates them and when they find out it's not true, it will destroy your future with this customer and his friends and family.

Major error:
Spill out all the benefits as fast as possible without keeping some as a reserve to handle any remaining objections (doubts).

Learn to engage your customer in a discussion of each advantage or benefit of the product. Find out how it helps him or how it handles a problem for him. Get him to participate in the conversation and get him to tell you how this will profit his life. Don't make the customer be a passive spectator of your "pitch." Customers will close themselves if you get them talking. Every good sales rep has heard this a million times, but it requires practice. Work on this skill every day, and both you and your customers will profit as a result. And you will have a lot more fun every day!

Advice № 39
Don't Create Confusion

There is a tendency of pressuring and overloading the customer with information, which results in the customer becoming less interested in the salesman and the product. The customer gets confused and overwhelmed, and then he walks away.

Look. Is the customer listening to you? You must always be observing the customer. Your success depends on knowing what's going on in the customer's mind, where is his attention, what is he thinking about. You don't need to read minds or make wild guesses.

Look and observe! You can tell if the customer is listening to you or not. You can tell if he is smiling or frowning or bored. Don't be so interested in your own pitch that you stop being interested in what is happening with the customer.

This seems obvious to some people, but go home or to a friend's house tonight and watch a few conversations. Watch the person speaking and the person "listening." Is the one talking even looking at the other? Can you tell when the person being talked "at" loses interest? This is not a hard skill to learn. But you must be willing to practice LOOKING!

It may amaze you to see something you never noticed before. You can always tell when the other person loses interest in your conversation. The trick is to notice it instantly and then do something about it. Ask a question to find out more information and get back on track. Don't waste your time or the customer's by droning on and on.

The main idea is to control his level of interest and to make sure that he is listening to you by observing his reactions while you talk. You find out what he is interested in by asking good questions and then give him the information he is interested in.

If you know your product and you've done your homework and researched the customer or asked enough questions to find out what the customer is looking for, you now know the customer's concerns and interests. Just start giving him easily understandable information on how he can handle his problem using your product or service.

If you didn't do any research or ask any questions about what he needs, you have to be very attentive. Most importantly, watch his eyes. If he looks away – even for a second – you should stop immediately and ask: *"Did you think of something?"*

Ask for details: *"What do you think about this?"* This is worth doing every time you suspect that you've lost his attention. Don't be afraid to make a mistake; it never hurts to ask what the customer is thinking about, they will tell you.

You should be aware of the customer's attention, because if you miss that moment, you will lose the customer. If this occurs and you don't notice, then you are talking *at* him and this will work against you. The result? The customer makes a decision: *"It's time to go and I have to find a good reason to get out of here, I hope he stops talking soon, because I'm not listening to him."* He will look around for this reason and he will listen for you to say something he disagrees with so he can leave quickly.

The error is:
Not paying attention to the customer's reactions while you are talking, and continue to load him with more information after that moment when the customer indicated he was no longer interested. Another rule is that sales reps tend to talk too much. Ask questions to get the customer talking!

Learn to keep your eyes on the customer while you are talking and the moment you notice the slightest indicator of the loss of attention or interest, you should ask him what is he thinking about and get him to tell you.

If you are on the phone, listen carefully. Listen for changes in his emotional tone and listen to background noises. On the phone you can't Look, but you sure can Listen. Get the customer talking. The customer will close himself, if you ask enough questions, and give him the exact information he needs to solve his problems.

Advice № 40
Sales Efficiency

Different sales reps have different levels of efficiency based on their closing effectiveness. These figures are based on the closing success of various types of sales reps. It is used to highlight the difference between an average sales rep and a Champion.

The lowest level of efficiency:
This type of sales rep tells the customer about all the benefits, barely stopping to take a breath. This level of efficiency equals 10%. Like a locomotive chugging down the track, making as few stops as possible. It's just not very effective. Most customers will hardly ever give you the opportunity to talk that much. Unfortunately, this is the level of the average sales rep in the world.

The next level of efficiency:
This level is 50%. This occurs when a sales rep asks questions about the customer's needs and experience, and listens to the answers. By listening, you sell! This is much more difficult than talking, because it "seems" that you can't sell if you don't talk! But listening is exactly the action that sells! Of course, you have to ask questions, but direct the questions at the discussion of problems, which can be solved using your product. And after you ask, you should listen and listen carefully. And then you ask more questions. At this stage each question, asked properly, hits the mark. Each question brings the customer more understanding of your product and service. Result - 50% effective or 5 times more effective than the average sales rep.

The highest level of efficiency:
This level is 100%. This occurs when a sales rep creates the customer's willingness to talk about advantages of the product or service for himself and then the customer finds out for himself that the product or service is really useful for him. If a person is interested in something, he will talk about it. So, get your customer telling *you* about the advantages, and he sells himself. Result - 100% effective! This is the level of the Champion.

Advice № 41
Demonstration

Demonstration is very important for the sales process and getting the customer to truly understand how your product or service will benefit them. Don't just talk about the advantages. Show them. If you sell face to face, it's easy: you just give the product to your customer and show how it works. But what do you do if you sell on the phone, or if you sell a service that can't be handled like an object? Don't neglect this important tool. It can be demonstrated! You may have to use your imagination, but it can be done and it makes your job much easier.

If it's a service, tell them how it is usually delivered, saving some of the benefits to show and demonstrate later. Take the installation of windows: your customer worries about damage to his house. You can show what actions are taken to protect the house during installation. Show recommendation letters from customers who specifically stated that no damage was done during their installation and how they benefitted from their new windows.

Another very effective method is to tell a story about how this advantage is being implemented or about how this product is being manufactured. While selling shoes or furniture, the best sales reps tell stories about the manufacturing process, the care taken, where the manufacturer is located, etc., in order to show how the important aspects were implemented. Stories are often used very successfully for creating emotional impact and demonstrating benefits for customers.

Advice № 42
Second-Rate

Why is saving money more important for some people than high quality? You may observe that many people will settle for less quality in the hope of saving some money. For some reason, many people will buy something that is not exactly what they really want, but it saves them money. Check it out yourself. We call this phenomenon a "Second-rate" purchase. For some reason, either to save money or because someone else said it was good enough, people settle for less.

Look in your closet and count how many pieces of clothing are hanging up that you never wear. "Second-rate" has a certain quality: *you don't really use it, but you can't seem to throw it away either.* It just hangs there, upsetting you from time to time. "Why did I buy that?"

Don't buy things you don't really like, even though it's "on sale!" A great sales rep is like "first-aid" in such cases. Learn how to show your customer the value of higher quality items and show how expensive "second-rate" items will be for him at the end of the day. Don't be afraid to ask the question: "Why would you waste your money to buy problems for yourself?" or "Why would you buy something that is not really what you want?" or "How expensive is it if you buy it and never use it?" or "How much money did you really save, if you never use it?"

Advice № 43
Help Make the Best Choice

The Art of Sales is all about helping the customer get the necessary information to make the best choice for the customer!

Let's break down this process systematically. What does this service to the customer consist of?

The Customer needs your help in the following areas:
- Getting *useful* information to help make the most logical decision from the customer's viewpoint;
- Proper distribution of priorities and evaluation of importance of those product qualities which are important for the customer and *based on his needs and experience*;
- Giving him enough information to make a decision which maximizes the future results and gives the customer maximum profit – *in spite of his desire to "save money."* It's very important to help him gain confidence that he is making the right decision and handle any doubts;
- Choosing the best form of payment and turning this decision into action.

The main function of a sales rep is to help the customer get through the steps above. This is what we expect from a Professional Sales Rep. Both your company and the customer are expecting this service. You can use the following phrase: *"Let me tell you about this and then we both will find out what is the most important benefit for you, and then you will make the best decision for you."*

Advice № 44
Asking Questions

Sales is the *service provided to help the customer make the best choice.* If you just remember this, "selling" is easy.

You could say that "selling" is providing information about the product benefits that can improve the customer's quality of life.

You discuss these positive qualities with the customer, *solely in terms of the future use and potential benefit <u>to the customer</u>*. How will your customer use the product or service to improve his life. The lack of understanding of this important benefit often misleads both customer and salesman. Why do people buy anything? So they can use it for their benefit!

And the customer must "win" while <u>using</u> your product. And your product should work exactly the way you described once he gets it home or back to the office.

Occasionally a customer comes to you and only wants to "save money," forgetful of how he will use the product. He just wants to save money. This is why a professional salesman is needed, to keep the customer from "losing" in the long run! You should never forget the customer's "profit" - *<u>even if the customer forgets</u>*. The customer's "profit" is based on the long-term benefits from using the product: the benefits must be greater than the upfront cost.

Remember this point!

Then you can create the correct relationship with the customer. And you will know how to ask the proper questions to get the customer to understand the long-term benefits based on the product's usefulness. The most important questions lead the customer to understand how and why he is going to use this product and what benefits the customer expects from using it. Your skillful questions influence the degree of trust in the future benefits.

Without "trust" the sale is impossible.

When you ask your customer what details he is looking for – color, form, function, etc. – you must look for qualities and benefits the customer forgets, because YOU are the expert in *using* this product, not the customer.

Advice № 45
Never be Afraid to "Lose" a Customer

This is a law.

Every Champion knows this law and applies it daily.

This is just how life works.

The highest paid sales reps know this is one of the basic rules of life in sales. You will not have a lot of happy customers if you cling to each prospect or if you are afraid to lose them or you are just afraid that they won't buy anything.

This is <u>very important</u>: *you should always be willing and able to just let the customer walk away.* This <u>doesn't</u> mean you want them to walk away empty handed. But, if you are willing and able to lose a customer, you won't lose many of them, as a rule. In fact, you will have many more customers who refer their friends and associates to you.

The most successful professionals constantly use this law. They know it's true. Please realize that this is not a trick or intrigue or swindle. This is simple truth. Champions are not afraid of refusals and they NEVER try selling something to somebody who doesn't need their product. That's why they have so many LOYAL customers, who constantly refer their friends and associates.

Advice № 46
Principle of Unsinkability

People tend to get very upset when they fail.

Have you ever seen this happen?

Has it ever happened to you?

What is the best way to handle this?

We have observed a few ways that people tend to handle failure:

1. Never stick your neck out. Do nothing, then you can never fail. Many people use this method.

    They don't do anything because they are afraid to fail. Example: a sales rep doesn't walk up to a customer in the shop because he has learned that "customers hate to be hassled by sales reps." Sales Reps tend to learn this lesson from a few disgruntled shoppers and then decide that the best thing to do is nothing. The store needs a good manager, who can show the proper way to approach people actively but effectively. It's not very difficult to train anyone how to do this.

2. Be upset on the inside, but pretend nothing has happened on the outside. People who tend to do this, build up internal pressure until they "crack" or "blow up."

    The point of "blow up" is called "critical mass" in physics. Enough failures accumulate, until for no apparent reason, you see the explosion. And if you look carefully, you can tell when a person is nearing *critical mass*: a strained smile, unnecessary chatter, fussiness, a sour look or sour words - "if you don't like it, don't buy it!" You probably remember times when you've seen these indicators around you and you knew instinctively to get out of the way.

3. Then there is the best way. We call it *the principle of unsinkability*. How does this work? Luckily, it's very simple. What is failure? It's something people don't want to deal with. People don't like to see it, hear it, or talk about it. For example, when somebody refuses to take your call, it can make you feel like a failure. Simply stated, a failure is anything that you don't want to be part of anymore.

Mistakes are not necessarily failures. If you learn from your mistakes, it becomes part of your education process and you continue to move forward. People who are actively trying to reach their goals make mistakes along the way. The trick is to learn from those mistakes and to continue to move toward your goal. Mistakes are part of living life. But it's very easy to turn mistakes into "failure." How? By refusing to look at the mistakes because it's too painful or uncomfortable. Some people would rather pretend everything's fine or nothing happened or it wasn't their fault. They are too worried about what others might think of them.

Those people who are busy "doing" something are making mistakes too and they don't have time to laugh at your mistakes. In fact, they understand, and will treat you respectfully, because they recognize that you are at least trying. But, if you insist on paying attention to the criticisms of the "unerring people" – the lazy cowards – you then start to back off from any mistake, avoid talking about it, and obviously as a result, there will be no lesson learned from your mistake. Then you become more and more afraid of making other mistakes, and the more you fear something, the more you get what you fear. This is simple truth.

If you don't want "failure", then learn to communicate with your mistakes and be willing to learn from them.

In sales, most mistakes result in the customer refusing to buy from you. Embrace the "mistake." Look at what happened exactly without blaming yourself or anyone else, find out how you could improve your handling of that customer, and learn from this failed close. Do that, and you will never be a "failure."

Decide to learn from your mistakes, instead of trying to explain why you had to make those mistakes and you will continue to improve. Embrace mistakes and learn from them so you don't repeat them. This makes you unsinkable! And only then will you become a Champion Closer!

Key principle of wealthy salesmen:

Communicate with each and every customer comfortably, confidently, never afraid of losing any customer, always willing to help a customer understand and let them walk away when necessary. Learn from your mistakes. UNSINKABILITY! This is one of the most important components of super successful sales reps!

Advice № 47
Four Things You *Should* Talk About

Professional "Sales" is the art of increasing the customer's knowledge about the product's benefits and enhancing the long-term value of the product from the customer's viewpoint, and as a result, getting fair payment from the customer in a timely manner.

Please note: the payment should result from the customer's willingness to take advantage of your offer, not to escape your "high-pressure" tactics. He should give you his money with pleasure. And, he will return to you and do it again and again, *and* he will refer his friends.

You will have a much higher closing percentage when you show your customer the advantages of the following four things:

1. *You and your company;*
2. *Your product information and knowledge of benefits and ability to communicate this effectively and increase the customer's certainty in making this decision;*
3. *The product itself as a solution for the customer's long term problems;*
4. *Further connection with your company.*

If you did a great job of explaining all four points above so the customer really understood but still didn't buy right now, you still "won" and you did your job, fully educating the customer on the best value for him. By focusing on giving the customer a perfect sales experience, your overall closing efficiency will continue to rise. But if you don't understand what a "win" actually is, and you assign yourself a "failure" too often, you can't help but feel like you're "losing," and you will stop "selling," and you will become extremely stressed.

It's not difficult for a winner to let a customer walk away without buying something, he just continues to repeat the successful actions as often as necessary, without worry, without stress or strain, and with a high closing rate.

Advice № 48
Appreciate What the Customer Gives To You

You should understand and respect the *stress* your customer is under during the sales process, especially at the very beginning and at the very end.   Making a decision is not always easy, and any actual purchase requires a decision be made... right now. Customers usually don't even understand what they are experiencing. If the customer feels that the sales rep understands and appreciates what they are going through, this "understanding" is often the most significant contribution to the customer's decision to buy at that moment.

The customer expects to get *valuable information in exchange for his time and attention.*   If the sales rep does not provide this valuable information, the rep may get the idea that he just "stole" the customer's time and attention. He may start to feel uncomfortable because he is not keeping up his end of the basic exchange, and then he becomes unwilling to continue talking to this customer.

If you continue to offer the customer very useful information, he will easily maintain his willingness to talk with you. If you provide clear and necessary information, not just meaningless fluff, and if the customer understands the value of this information from his viewpoint, then you will feel no discomfort, and you will both enjoy the time you spend talking with each other, whether he chooses to buy something right now or not.

Fatal error:
Stop wasting your customer's time and attention by chattering nonsense, throwing worn out sales phrases and "closing" patter at him.

The customer gives his attention and time and expects to receive something valuable in exchange. Your information is valuable when it actually serves the customer's needs.

Let's assume you have a product of high quality and a corresponding high price.

Salesmen are constantly pounded on by customers with a simple phrase: "it's too expensive!" This is normal! This is the sales profession. Customers always say: "it costs too much!" Having heard this too many times, and too often failing to prove that it's *not* too expensive, the salesman may start to believe *every* customer is going to say this. So, he trains himself to be ready for this. He literally prepares for the "Cold War" with every customer. Pretending to be friendly, but ready to fight at a moment's notice. He doesn't keep his attention on all his product benefits - instead he prepares to fight against all the drawbacks including the "High Price." As soon as he starts thinking this way, there are no more advantages in his mind, just rebuttals against the expected objections.

The Ugly Duckling, by Hans Christian Andersen is still an appropriate story today. The "ugly duckling" was actually a baby swan. But the ducks and geese made him believe that he was no good and he didn't belong anywhere. What did that ugly duckling decide when he came up to the lake and saw the other swans? "They will probably kill me because I'm so ugly... Well... Let them..."

The same is true with a salesman. Everything is basically fine with him, he's a smart and competent person. But without the actual sales skills fully understood and drilled to perfection, he doesn't believe that everything is fine, and he goes to each customer with the attitude: "I will have to prove it to them or I'll fail!" Even experienced salesmen can act like this, suffering from this phenomenon of not knowing just how good their product or service is. They listened to their prospects and other average sales reps tell them how bad it is, how expensive it is, how they are never going to be successful selling it.

The best way to fully handle this phenomenon is for salesmen to act like professionals and to train so well, that they know all the benefits and advantages of their product or service and constantly and *systematically* prove to their own satisfaction, all the benefits and successes of the customers who have used their product or service.

Training and practice is how Champion Sales Reps are made and they never forget they are SWANS.

Advice № 50
Always Think of the Future

The role of a salesman is to help create steady growth and development of their company. New prospects, recommended by existing customers, are one of the main indicators of the success and prosperity of your sales team and your company. And there are also potential customers who found out about your product or service but didn't buy anything yet. They will come back and buy, depending on how well the sales professionals do their job.

What does any customer want from a salesman?

What do *you* want when you are buying something as a customer?

How do you want to be treated during the sales process when you are trying to buy something? You want your problem solved the best way for you, right? Not just the cheapest product or service, but the best value for your long-term future. You might want to be comfortable talking to the salesman, not feeling forced into a decision you aren't sure of. You probably want them to respect your power of choice, and give you enough information to make a "smart" decision, not the "cheapest" decision. How do you feel as a customer when a salesman fails to tell you about all the options, even if they are more expensive? How do you feel about the salesman when you get home and find out you saved some money, but the quality is nowhere near what you thought it would be?

Don't fall into the trap of "cheaper is always better." It is not true and does not lead to long-term customer satisfaction.

Advice № 51
First and Second Mistakes

According to the survey data, people remember and return again to those sales professionals who:

- Treated the customer with respect and educated them versus forcing them to buy.
- Didn't recommend the product if they realized it didn't really fit the customer's needs.
- Got the customer to understand that a more expensive product that was of higher long-term quality *actually was* the better option for the customer.
- Gave additional valuable information about their product or service: for example, they showed how to use all the benefits of the product and gave them a follow-up call to make sure they were satisfied.

We can easily remember salesmen like this. In fact, there is a fairly common way to find sales reps like this. We ask our friends and family: "Where did you buy your cell phone? Do you trust them? Did you get a Good Deal?" Remember, a "Good Deal" does not always mean the lowest price.

The *first* mistake would be to sell your customer something they don't really need or that doesn't fully solve their problem. This mistake causes most of the "returned" items and commission chargebacks. Avoid this mistake and your chargebacks will disappear.

The *second* mistake separates the average sales rep from the Champion. When the sales rep knows the customer needs a higher quality and more expensive solution to create a long-term benefit, but doesn't take the time and energy to really get the customer to understand the full situation, he is letting that customer down.

Champions persist, and are willing to communicate enough and take enough action and have enough courage to get the customer to understand the truth of long-term quality and value. Champions have high referral rates and customers that continually come back to purchase other items or services.

Champions also consistently get customers to understand and pay extra for high quality products and services. This is exactly why Champions make a LOT more money than the average sales rep.

Advice № 52
Truth about Customers

"Customers know everything about the product already, they are not interested in more information. They only want the lowest price!" Sales reps say this to their managers all the time, all over the world, in many different languages. It's a great excuse for not closing customers who say they are just price shopping.

The truth is, that people love to learn more about the things they are interested in. They appreciate the professional sales reps who care enough to take the time to teach them and they will refer their friends to these professionals over and over again.

People love to understand something that they didn't understand before. This is often hidden because they may feel bad that they don't already know and they are in no hurry to display their lack of understanding. By getting the customer to fully understand your product's benefits, or how it solves problems related to them, you immediately make the customer your friend.

One of the most common customer complaints per survey is sales rep incompetence.

In defense, sales reps assert: "Well, I do know what I'm talking about!" The problem is: *if **you** understand, but the customer doesn't understand, he will say that "you" are incompetent! Doesn't seem fair does it? He doesn't understand, and somehow it is your fault? So you must take the time to practice asking the customer questions to find the customer's interest and then fill in details related to your product that relate to their interest until they do understand. The customer "learns" something new, and then gives you all the credit for informing them.*

People love to talk about things they understand. This is exactly how you create free promotion for yourself. Customers who learn from you will tell others to come see you. Even if they didn't pay you right now, you made them into an ally. Get them to understand something fully and it will pay dividends to you for a long time to come.

Advice № 53
Ideas which Prevent Sales

Here is a common complaint from sales reps: "I spend the time to educate the customer, and then they go and buy it somewhere else for less."

According to actual experience, people tend to go to places where they feel good. A person will come back to the same place over and over. This rule is not canceled by low or high prices. This rule does not submit to the laws of logic. Emotions have their own laws!

The atmosphere of any place where you felt good, will call you back, and you go there even if your logic tells you that you can save money elsewhere.

This is where the false idea of having to "pressure" people by arguing with them comes in to play. This idea assumes that you are in a "fight" with the customer.

This is the "Cold War" between the customer and the salesman.

Argument is a reason or set of reasons that you use to persuade others that they are wrong and you are right. This position assumes there is a fight and one person will win and one person will lose.

But the truth is, that the *sale is a very emotional thing* from start to finish.

People don't buy goods and services.

People buy:
- emotions
- thoughts
- imagination
- feelings
- expectations
- anticipated rewards

And customers will pay their hard earned money for these valuable ideals.

Don't lose this advantage for your company and yourself. Sometimes businesses without commissioned salesmen appear more attractive to the average customer. But a business like this normally attracts less competent salesmen from other companies. A "Professional" salesman is a significant advantage for any company. This is a fact.

Sales Professionals know that customers buy on emotion much more often than logic. They buy because they are afraid to lose something. They pay more in some places because they like the way they are treated. They buy because they fully understand and feel safe in their decision that their long-term goals will be met. The professional uses all these feelings combined with excellent product knowledge to make it safe for the customer to buy _now_.

Advice № 54
Fall in Love with Your Product

What does a great sales rep do? He gradually, step by step, communicates the value of his proposition to the customer. He displays the appropriate benefits of his product and gets the customer to fully understand that the value of the proposition is greater than the cost. But is it really clear to you that you really need to believe in the value of your proposition first? To communicate effectively, you should believe in what you are selling!

YOU SHOULD FALL IN LOVE WITH YOUR PRODUCT AND YOUR COMPANY IN ORDER TO BE WILDY SUCCESSFUL.

Every time a customer has experienced dealing with a sales rep, who is truly passionate about his company and product, they walk away imbued with a portion of that passion.

If the value of a product grows in the customer's mind after the sales rep contacts him, it means the sales rep did his job correctly.

Rule:

You either increase or decrease the value of your product in the customer's mind while you talk to him. The more you love your company and product, the more likely you are to increase the value and increase his willingness to deal with your company in the future.

Best of all, you will find that this customer will communicate your passion to his friends and family, increasing your commission with less effort on your part.

Advice № 55
Wealthy Sales Reps

Have you ever been completely enthusiastic about a new idea?

How do you feel about it?

How do you talk about it?

You should be ready to talk for hours about YOUR PRODUCT or SERVICE:
how it's manufactured, its benefits, how to use it, about your company and how it was founded, and any other interesting details about your product.

Your product and your company should INSPIRE you. You should be able to be completely ENTHUSIASTIC about it. You should be DEDICATED to your product, your company and your job. You should be INTERESTED in your profession every day. You should be willing to be a professional, which requires study and practice.

ONLY after you have decided that you like your own product, service and company, will any other sales techniques really work for long-term success.

Learning techniques in order to sell a product you don't like will ultimately lead to hating your product, your job and even your profession. You will "push away" more customers than you attract.

Most importantly:

If you can't develop passion for your product and company, if you don't believe in the value of your product, you will tend to limit your own pay, whether you are aware of this principal or not. And you will tend to attract customer objections, even if they didn't have any objections in the first place.

In order to be a "Wealthy Sales Professional" you have to sell a

101

product you believe in and work for a company you can be proud of. It's your choice what you sell and who you work for. Choose wisely. Your success depends on your choice. Your happiness in this profession depends on your choice. Also, you can take responsibility for improving your product and your company. That may take more courage. It's up to you.

Be a Champion.
Find your passion. Tell others about your passion.
Practice, Practice, Practice!
Use the Sales Drills in the course book.
You **_can_** be a Wealthy Sales Champion.

We wish you all the best!
Andrey and Jim

Summer of 1985: Andrey was hunting American Nuclear Submarines as a Lieutenant on a Russian Anti-Submarine Corvette operating in the North Atlantic Ocean.

Jim was a Lieutenant aboard USS Flying Fish, SSN 683. The mission was to hunt down Russian Ballistic Missile Submarines operating in the North Atlantic Ocean.

In essence, Andrey was hunting Jim and Jim was hunting Andrey's friends (Russian Submarine Captains).

Map Image Credit: U.S. Geological Survey
Department of the Interior/USGS

Fall of 1985: Jim's submarine (USS Flying Fish, SSN 673) was operating in the Mediterranean Sea hunting Russian Ballistic Missile Submarines.

Map Image Credit: U.S. Geological Survey
Department of the Interior/USGS

Photo Credit: wikimedia.org Public Domain

USS Flying Fish (SSN-673) at sea 1972
Jim Mathers served on the Flying Fish from May 1985 until May 1988.

It's cold up near the North Pole.

Russian Anti Submarine Corvette
Albatross Class
Lt. Andrey Sizov, Weapons Officer
http://www.zamotiviruy.ru/

Nanuchka Class Corvette similar to Andrey's corvette

Typical training exercise performed by Andrey's crew in the North Sea during the Cold War circa 1985.

Yes, that is frozen ice all over the ship. Russian sailors are tough! Obviously, Andrey had a much "colder" Cold War than Jim did inside his cozy submarine.

Jim with a couple of his classmates visiting the US Naval Academy in 1988.

From left to right: Marine Captain, Jeff Fletcher with his sons, Surface Warfare Officer, Lt. Sean "Sonny" O'Connor, and Submarine Warfare Officer, Lt. Jim Mathers.

All 3 were 1983 graduates of the US Naval Academy.

2013, Jim Mathers, Vlad Musatov, and Andrey Sizov. Jim and Andrey were guest speakers at Vlad's summer conference in St Petersburg, Russia.

Andrey delivering motivational seminar in Kiev, 2015.

Andrey in Kiev, 2015

Andrey: having fun in Kiev, 2015.

Jim with Grant and Elena Cardone in Moscow, 2014. Jim and Grant addressed nearly 1000 Russian business owners and managers on Sales and Marketing secrets.

Moscow, 2014: Listening to Grant Cardone enlighten and entertain at the same time.

Andrey and Jim with Russian business leaders in Moscow 2014

Jim was guest speaker in St Petersburg, Russia, 2014

St Petersburg Russia, 2015: Jim's translator, Tanya Markova

Jim in Moscow's Red Square, 2014.

Jim & Andrey in Moscow, 2014

Jim & Andrey, St Petersburg, 2012

Jim & Fu Mei Mathers with Andrey and Elena Sizov, St Petersburg, 2012

Leadership Award, 2012

Jim in Taipei, Taiwan; Moonlight Sales Seminar, 2012

Jim & Andrey in St Petersburg, 2013

Moscow awards ceremony; 2012

After Seminar in Riga, Latvia, 2012

We want <u>You</u> to Succeed beyond your wildest dreams!!!!

Is a New Cold War Inevitable?
Tensions rise as Russia rattles her nuclear saber to rival Cold War levels.

Mobile intercontinental ballistic missile launchers being sent to a testing range near Moscow in February, 2015. *PHOTO: VLADIMIR SMIRNOV/ ZUMA PRESS*

Jim and Andrey believe that good communication skills and proper negotiation fundamentals will help to prevent a war between the USA and Russia and China.

Jim giving Sales Training to his friends in St Petersburg, Russia, 2014.

The reason we included all these photos of our friends around the world is to point out one important thing. These people are people. They are hard working men and women.

In fact, it's hard to tell Russians and Ukrainians and Americans apart, as long as we all just smile at each other and don't open our mouths.

If we take language out of the equation, we could be friends very easily. Which proves that with effective communication, any problem can be solved without fighting.

Yes! We are optimistic about the future. And we wish to share that optimism with our friends on all continents, not just Russia and USA.

We hope to see you soon!

Best wishes for your success!
Jim & Andrey

Made in the USA
Middletown, DE
20 August 2015